FOR ANNE

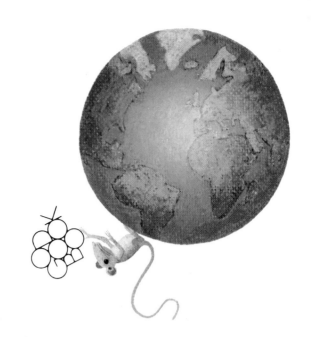

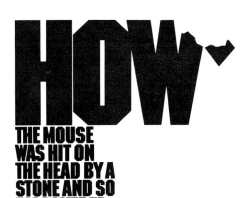

HOW

THE MOUSE WAS HIT ON THE HEAD BY A STONE AND SO DISCOVERED THE WORLD

TEXT AND PICTURES BY ETIENNE DELESSERT FOREWORD BY JEAN PIAGET

In collaboration with
Odile Mosimann for the text
and experimentation

Director of experimentation:
Professor
Jean Piaget, Geneva
Collaborator in the
experimentation: Anne
van der Essen, Lausanne
Foreword translated by
Kenneth Grinling, Geneva
Text translated by
C. Ross Smith, New York
Editor: John Ernst, New York
Organization and coordi-
nation: Anne van der Essen
and Bertil Galland,
Lausanne
Designer: Etienne
Delessert, New York
Art direction:
Herb Lubalin and Etienne
Delessert, New York
Production director:
Jean Genoud, Lausanne
Designer of display type:
Tom Carnase, New York
Photographs: Marcel Imsand,
Lausanne and Paul
Hosefros, New York
We wish to express our
thanks for the help of
the Ecoles enfantines
of the City of Lausanne

Color separations by Ast
and Jakob, Koeniz-Bern
Printed in Switzerland
by Offset Jean Genoud S.A.
Lausanne
Bound by A. Horowitz
& Son, Clifton, New Jersey

Produced by Good Book, Inc.,
New York
Doubleday & Company, Inc.,
Garden City, New York

Foreword

Etienne Delessert is a well-known and talented artist whose illustrations are admired by the expert for their striking qualities of line and color and by the simple psychologist, unversed in the field of art, for their surprising combination of a sense of well-being and love of life, nonconformity, acute observation, unfailing humor, and a gentle irony that at times can be almost cruel, so neatly does it strike just where most needed. In other words, Etienne Delessert gives the impression of a highly intelligent and skillful adult who has managed to retain the principal traits of a child's mind with all its fantasy and unpredictable imagination and also its faculty for sharp observation applied where least expected. It was natural that, sooner or later, Delessert should come to writing and illustrating books for children, and this is what he has now done for five- and six-year-olds.

What is remarkable in so intuitive an artist is that, before starting, he wished to find out just how children of that age-group comprehend the world about them and interpret the details of observable phenomena. This was not simply the natural desire of an author of children's books to make sure beforehand that his text and illustrations would interest his young readers and, more important, be understood by them. If that were all, Etienne Delessert would still deserve high praise, for few writers and even fewer illustrators are so scrupulous. But his ambition went further. What he set out to do was to write and illustrate a book based on the ideas that children express in response to systematic questioning. I had worked along these lines many years earlier for my studies on "The Child's Conception of the World" and "The Child's Conception of Physical Causality," and that is why Etienne Delessert came to me for help in carrying out his project.

I was naturally interested in the idea, but also somewhat embarrassed for a reason that I shall explain. The book in your hands is not in the least intended to present and to illustrate the child's "serious" ideas – those he really believes in and arrives at through an effort of his intelligence to understand a particular phenomenon that has aroused his curiosity; for example, how the sun, moon, clouds, or wind were or are still being made, how they move and how they behave. Still less does it seek to "educate" the child by virtue of the insights furnished by child psychology. What it aims at is to be a children's book like any other, but if possible better than most because better adapted to its audience. It sets out simply to amuse and to interest, and to do so by mixing imagination and observation, while catering to the child's artistic needs and keeping the proposed text and illustrations at his level of understanding. It does this, first, by taking certain ideas of young children, transposing them esthetically, making them more exciting, and even exaggerating them if need be, all of which may make a child smile and awaken his critical sense, but may equally well seem to him quite natural in a book read for fun.

To take examples from my early work, several children in the four to six age-group told me that the sun and moon were "made" by a gentleman who lighted them up, that the rain came from a sort of reservoir in the sky, while the clouds were made of smoke but carried the rain, etc. Delessert's drawings take up themes of this kind but give them such an enchanting and concrete form that it is difficult to say where an interpretation acceptable to the child ends and the fantasy begins. It was similarly difficult, in the children's sayings that I collected, to distinguish what was believed from what was invented on the spur of the moment or put in for the simple pleasure of embroidering.

My difficulty, then, was to know what to advise. My early work had been concerned with the ideas spontaneously expressed by children on subjects such as these, but not with their esthetic sense or their reactions – whether of amusement, imagination, or understanding – to picture books.

I decided therefore to set up a piece of research together with Etienne Delessert and with the collaboration of Odile Mosimann, a good psychologist experienced in working with children. Twenty-three children between five and six years of age were questioned to discover what they thought of the proposed story and pictures. Delessert and Odile

Photo: A work session. From left to right: Odile Mosimann, Etienne Delessert, Jean Piaget and Anne van der Essen.

Mosimann first prepared a provisional and, in a way, experimental text together with drawings that were also of an experimental nature. Odile Mosimann examined the children concerning these, giving three sessions to each child. The children's reactions were carefully analyzed and used in preparing the final text and illustrations.

The book tells the story of a little mouse living under the ground with his parents. The mouse decides to dig a tunnel in order to make a room of his own. Suddenly the roof caves in and when the dazed little mouse opens his eyes he is looking at the sun, with whom he begins a conversation. Later he also talks to the night, the clouds, the moon, etc. This leads to a series of questions and answers that are freely borrowed from my records of what children actually said when questioned by me forty years ago, but presented in the most charming and fanciful way. In the book, they are put into the mouths of the mouse and the other actors in a sort of play whose characters are personifications of natural phenomena.

What we did, then, was first to read the text, passage by passage, to the children (five- or six-year-olds usually cannot read) to see if they understood the meaning or had difficulties with the vocabulary, the construction of sentences, or the phrasing. Next we tried to discover whether the details of the story were really believed or accepted as fiction; hence the questions "Do you understand?," "What does that mean?," and so forth, were followed by others relating to particular passages in the story: "Is that what you think yourself, or not?," "Why not?," "Do you like that part?," and so forth. Then we had the children tell what they remembered a week later, for memories, whether exact or distorted, are most revealing both of the child's comprehension and of the amount of interest he has taken in the story.

The children were also questioned about the pictures. This was done in three stages. First, without any reference to a text, they were shown pictures from three of Delessert's earlier books, two of which contained illustrations of stories written by Ionesco. It was an agreeable surprise to find that sometimes the children had no trouble, and even took pleasure, in distinguishing the various animals, persons, or objects represented, and also that when they looked at a picture they were able to discover exactly what the artist intended to convey – for instance the expressions of curiosity, amazement, or humor portrayed by this or that character. Furthermore, drawings that were deliberately out of proportion did not disturb the children, nor were they frightened by pictures of "monsters," unless adults stressed their wickedness. The imaginary or the fanciful does not worry a child as long as the elements in a surrealistic situation are drawn in a sharp, clear, and unambiguous way. It would seem, therefore, that the range of techniques and subjects open to the artist goes far beyond the narrow limits within which many authors of over-sweet children's books are content to remain. Etienne Delessert can certainly not be accused of this common defect.

With regard to the pictures intended for the present work, the children were questioned in two ways. First they were shown the artist's sketches for various parts of the story – the flower and the shadow, the formation of rain, the moon theme. Those who were unacquainted with the story were asked what the pictures were about; others were asked whether the pictures were good illustrations of the part of the text they had listened to. Lastly, the children themselves were invited to make a drawing to illustrate a passage that had just been read to them.

Although modest in scope, these various preparatory tests for the book that I have the pleasure to present to the reader have produced most instructive results. However, since they were carried out in only one town of French-speaking Switzerland, it cannot be assumed that similar reactions would have been obtained elsewhere.

We were able to make sure that the proposed pictures were well understood and were considered adequate illustrations of the corresponding passages in the text. It was still more pleasing to discover that the pictures made by the children themselves resembled Delessert's sketches, often to a striking

Photo: Etienne Delessert and one of the children who took part in the research.

degree. This confirms what I said before about his remaining young enough to be able, on occasion, to rediscover the five- or six-year-old child's vision of the world–a gift equally necessary to the artist and the psychologist.

It goes without saying that some of the expressions used in the text had to be corrected because they were not understood or were considered wrong by the child. Examples are "grâce à moi," "depuis que," and "faire connaissance."* The use of the verb "to plant" applied to a flower and to a stone was found wrong, and one child aged five years and eleven months pointed out that "for flowers you put in little seeds, and for stones you take an axe and hammer them in." As for the ideas expressed, each child will, of course, assimilate them in terms of his own experience or his own conceptions, and will approve or disapprove accordingly. Among the ideas rejected may be mentioned the following supposition that I had noted many years before from a little girl of four, although whether she really believed it is very difficult to say: "It's the breathing of grown-ups that makes the wind." This notion was turned down by all the children questioned by Odile Mosimann, and was therefore deleted from the text. The idea that the sky and the clouds were made of stones stuck together was vigorously refused also. One child five and one-half years of age commented, "I don't see any stones–the sky can't be made out of stones, it's built out of clouds," and a six-year-old dismissed the idea thus: "Those big stones are just clouds." The passage in question was therefore changed to "The sky is made of tightly-packed little clouds." However, there was a certain amount of agreement about how the moon becomes all round again: "They make it all round again, big strong people that go with parachutes." The obvious reference to some scrap of information about astronauts should put us on our guard–today's child knows about things that it was impossible to know about forty years ago. This is reflected also in the following protest from a child aged six years and three months: "The moon is too big to go all around it and stick the half back on." Yet, however much the information that the child acquires from adults has changed in recent years, there still remains some common ground. With regard to the relations between sky, clouds, and wind, for example, a six-year-old girl told us: "There are also blue clouds; you see them in fine weather," or "It's the clouds that make the wind; they start the wind and when it blows it moves the sky a little," or again "The shadow comes up to the root [of the flower] to give it food," as if the shadow were a substance acting causally.

Generally speaking, the children were keenly interested in the story told them and sometimes even laughed a lot. From one session to the next they remembered, often very well, what had been read to them. Occasionally they made fresh suggestions that were accepted.

Such were the preliminary investigations called for by this book. They do not, of course, authorize any very new psychological conclusions regarding the child's esthetic feelings, although in the reactions we obtained to Delessert's delightful book, we do find two of the components of the play of a child's imagination–the need to relate to reality and the need to transcend reality so that the powers of the characters concerned are enhanced. Even less can any pedagogical conclusions be drawn from these investigations; indeed that was never their objective. The two things that stand out in this admirable adventure of an artist seeking to create the best possible book for children of five to six years of age are the author's immense talent and, above all, the remarkable professional integrity that led him conscientiously to adapt himself to his young readers instead of simply trusting to his intuition. In so doing, he has avoided the dangers of an "adult-centered" attitude that is as damaging in art as it is in psychology. He is to be most warmly congratulated on his work, whose worth and originality must be obvious to all.

Jean Piaget
Geneva, February 1971

Drawing: Portrait of the mouse by a child five years and four months of age.

* The corresponding English expressions "thanks to me," "since," used as a conjunction, and "make acquaintance" would not necessarily give rise to the same difficulties.

"I am a mouse.
I am five years old
and I have lived for a long time
in an underground house
with my Mommy and Daddy.
I have never
been outside my house
and it is so small
that there is not much
room to play."

The mouse decides to build a room all his own. Mommy and Daddy agree, saying: "That's a very good idea. You can make it yourself. If the work gets too difficult, we can help."

The mouse already knows how to dig the ground. "First," he says to himself, "I will make a tunnel." He starts scratching in front of him, scraping away the earth with his paws. The work is slow. The mouse digs for fifteen minutes, a long time when you are that small. "Ooh!" he cries. His back aches. He wants to sit down, but he cannot. There is no room. The tunnel is too low and the earth crushes him on every side.

"I will have to make the tunnel bigger," the mouse thinks.

He digs on all sides: in front of him, behind, underneath, above. The earth is hard, and there are roots and sharp pebbles everywhere.

The mouse is very tired. His paws hurt. Oh, if only he could find some nice loose earth.

The mouse rests for a moment, shakes his fur, and cleans his whiskers. Then he begins a new tunnel.

This time he finds looser earth and it is easy for him to dig. The new tunnel curves uphill and down. After a while he turns back along the tunnel to admire his work. Then he slides down it again as if on a toboggan. He enjoys the sliding so much that for a moment he forgets about making his room.

Going back to work, he starts scratching at the tunnel's ceiling, and with one of his paws tries removing a big stone. Suddenly, the stone falls on his head. He is blinded, scared. When he opens his eyes, he is dazzled by a great light. What is happening? He hears a noise and sticks his head outside the hole. There he sees a strange sight indeed.

"Hello, who are you?" the mouse asks. "I've never seen you before."

"I am the sun."

"Are you the one who is hurting my eyes?"

"Yes, because I shine so brightly. I am a ball of fire."

"Do please move back," says the mouse. "And tell me again who you are."

"I am the sun, and I am very old. I came a long time ago, about the same time as mice. Before that, there was nothing to light. I warm those who are cold and make those who are hot thirsty. During the day, I am the one who makes light."

"It's true," says the mouse, "I see that now. You light me. How strange! My coat is all gray."

For the first time, the mouse can see his fur and paws.

"How did you start shining?" the mouse asks.

"Once a gentleman lit me with a huge match," the sun answers. "Every morning he throws me high in the sky, and I shine; but in the evening he catches me again. Then night takes my place."

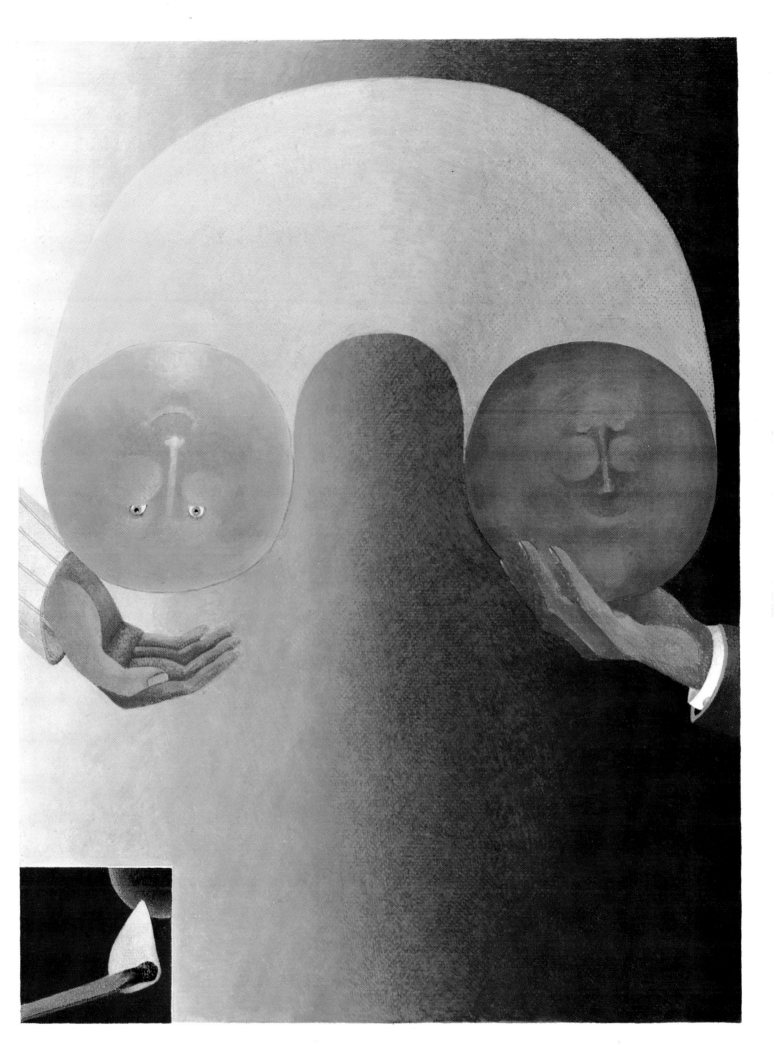

"Who is night?" asks the mouse.

"I am the night," a deep voice answers.

"I already know you," says the mouse. "You are as black as ink. I saw you underground in my parents' house."

"Yes, I go underground. I also go above ground and to the sky," night says.

"What is the sky?" the mouse asks.

"The sky is made of tightly-packed little clouds that are blue in daytime and black at night. I live in the sky with the sun, but I never meet the sun because I go to bed when he gets up. I am the one who brings sleep. I make people sleep because I bring the darkness with me, like a huge black cloud."

"But I waken everyone," says the sun.

"Not everyone," says the mouse. "It's hunger that wakes me up. But night was talking about clouds. Can I see a cloud now?"

"Here I am," says the cloud. "I am like smoke from chimneys and pipes, and like flying dust. Sometimes I am white, sometimes I am gray. I wander about the sky. As the wind blows, it pushes me and it changes my shape. If I bump against another cloud, I make a sound like a hammer: That is thunder."

"Oh, show me how you bump against other clouds," the mouse cries.

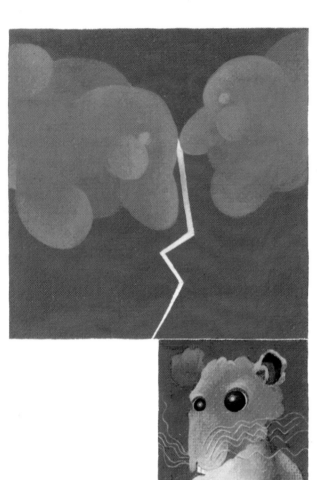

To please the mouse, the cloud lunges against another cloud. A great lightning flash lights the sky; thunder rumbles grandly.

The mouse is very impressed. His whiskers curl in surprise.

The cloud laughs. "I can do many other things as well," he says. "Now I want you to meet the rain."

The wind blows, whipping up waves like mountains, and the cloud drops down to the sea. Sliding, rolling, bouncing on every wave, it swallows a lot of water. It grows and swells until it is enormous.

The wind blows harder still, gradually making the huge cloud rise into the sky where other smaller clouds cluster around it, asking, "How did you become so big?" Very proud indeed, the big cloud gives each smaller one some of its own water. Then all of them make a great raining together.

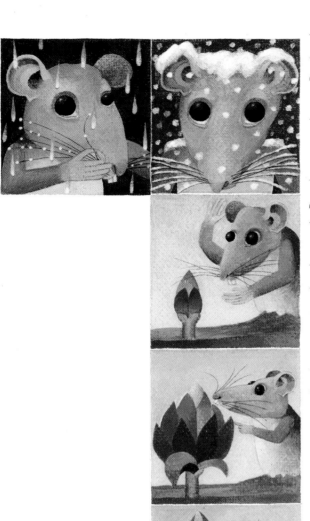

The mouse is delighted; drops of water shine on his whiskers.

"Since you are having such fun," says the cloud, "here is another surprise. I will ask the wind to help me again."

The wind begins blowing very hard on the rain, and it becomes white. "That is the snow!" the cloud says. "It is beautiful but cold."

The mouse shivers.

"Enough!" the cloud says to the wind. "Hold your breath!" Then he shouts to the other clouds: "The playing is now over!"

The mouse leans down to sniff the delicious odor of wet earth. When he raises his head again, he notices a curious pink and green object there, very close.

"What a funny little root!" cries the mouse. "Where did you come from?"

The curious little pink and green object is annoyed. "I am not a root," it says. "I am a flower. When I was planted, I was nothing but a little seed. But the rain made me grow."

The flower grows so quickly that its petals are already opening. The mouse has to raise his head, now, in order to look at it.

"Surely I am prettier than a mere root," says the flower, bowing its head so that the mouse can admire it.

The mouse thrusts his snout among the petals and smells a sweet perfume.

"You are a lovely flower," says the sun, "but without me, you would lose your colors."

"That may be," the flower says. "But I also need some shade so that I won't be burned up. Hey, little mouse, take your snout away! Your whiskers tickle me. Let me show you my shadow instead."

The flower straightens itself. But where is the shadow hiding? Just above the flower, the sun bursts out laughing. "Wait! I am the one who makes shadows."

The sun backs off a little, and the shadow appears at the foot of the flower.

"It's like a slice of almost-night," says the mouse. "How funny! It looks like the flower."

"Look in front of you," says the flower. "You will see a shadow that looks like a mouse! There is a shadow of a flower and a shadow of a mouse."

"It's hard to understand that the shadow doesn't come from the night," says the mouse.

"I hear someone talking about me," says the night in a sleepy voice. "When I hear my name, I waken. It's very peaceful here with my friends the moon and the stars. They never disturb my sleep."

"I would love to meet your friends," says the mouse.

"Well then, close your eyes," the night answers. "I will count to three. One, two, three…"

"Here I am," says the moon. "I'm as old as the sun. Often I am round, but tonight I'm only half myself. I wear out, you know. It's hard to light the dark. I move when the wind pushes me."

"How do you become round, again?" the mouse asks.

"A gentleman fetches my other half," the moon says. "He makes me round again."

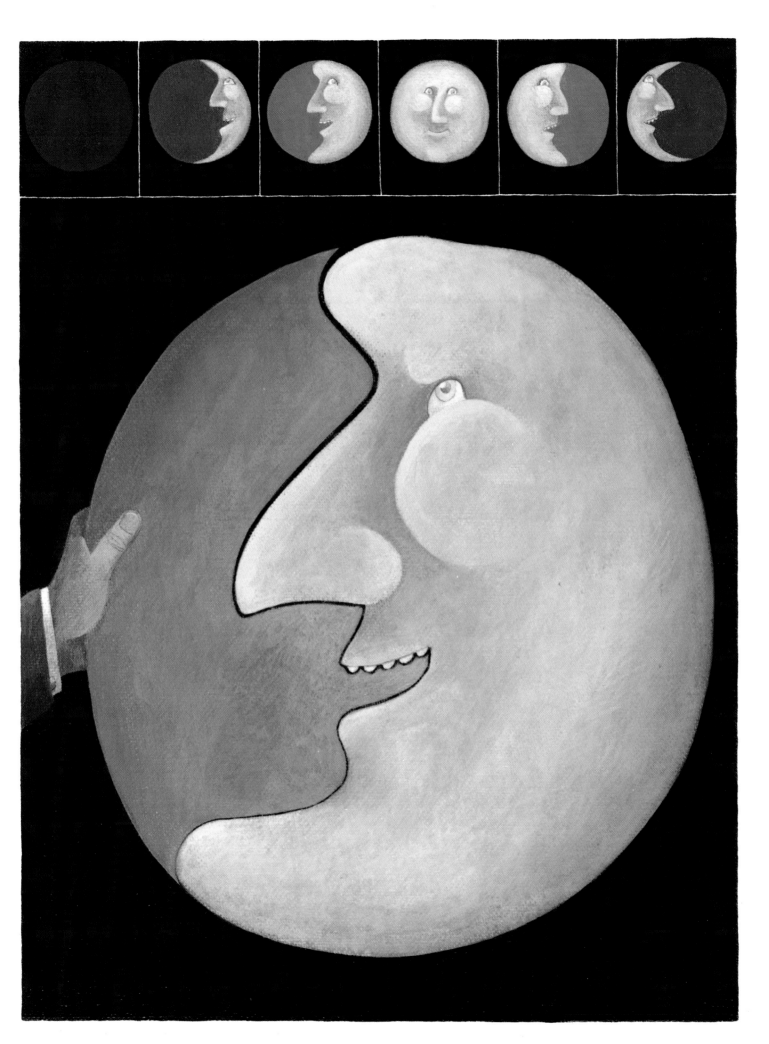

"And those little lights all around you, what are they?" the mouse asks. "Bits of moon?"

"No, those are stars," the moon answers. "Stars are little sparks that have gathered together. They shine in the night like cats' eyes."

"I heard my name again," says the night. "How pleasant. I like being talked about. I am so beautiful..."

"Don't listen," the moon says to the mouse. "Without me and the stars, the night would be just an ugly black cloud."

"Stop quarreling!" the mouse cries. "Let me tell you something. I think the night is beautiful and the moon, too. I love the stars, and I would like to fall asleep counting them. And you, flower, you smell so good. I also love playing with shadows. I can make little shadows and big ones, too, when the sun shines.

Sun, you are the strongest: You warm the earth and make the day light, and you even give the flower its colors.

I love all of you! You are all my friends!"

"Today you met us," says the sun. "Tomorrow you will have many other friends, but you will have to leave home to find them. You must take a long trip."

So the sun turns to the cloud, the thunder, the lightning, the rain, the wind, the snow, the flower, the shadow, the night, the moon, and the stars, and says to them: "Let's each give the mouse a going-away present. What do you think?"

"Yes, yes, yes, yes, yes, yes, yes, yes, yes, yes, yes," the sun's friends answer. "Good idea! Let's get a sack!"

Each puts his present in the sack: a small piece of sun, a wisp of cloud, a rumble of thunder, a flash of lightning, a raindrop, a gust of wind, a snowflake, a flower petal, a touch of shade, a slice of night, a crescent moon, and a tiny star.

Very pleased, the mouse thanks his new friends.

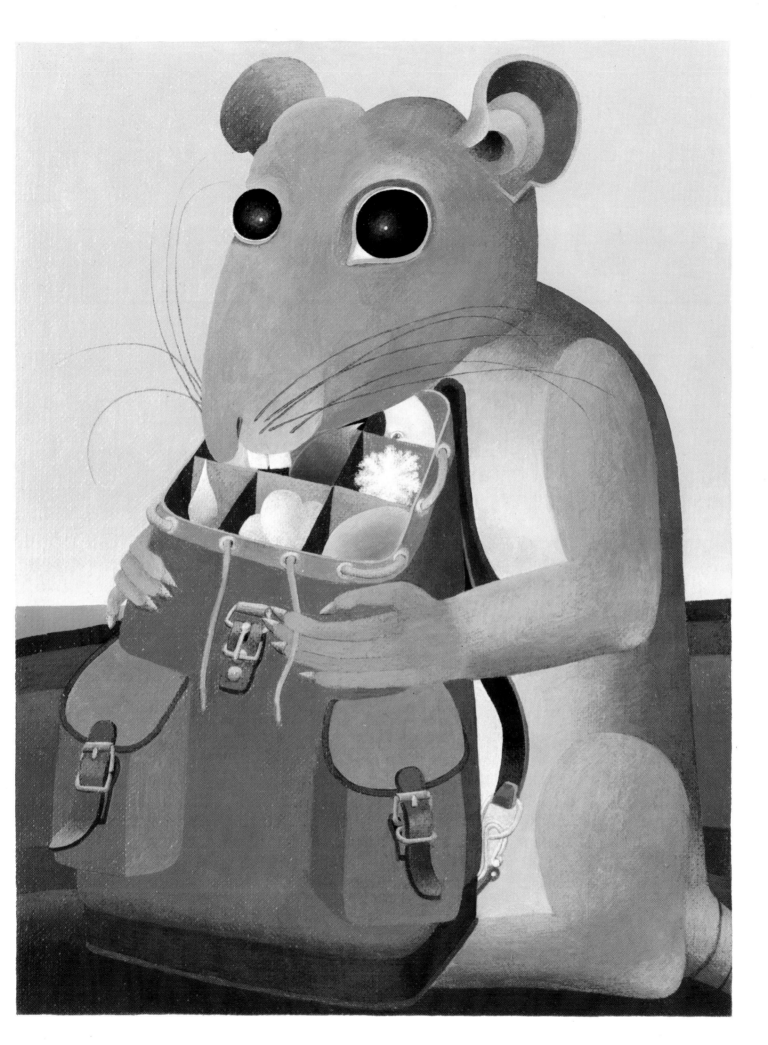

Then the mouse comes all the way out of his hole. He puts the sack on his back and sets out to follow the sun.

The sun and the mouse are going for a long trip on
which they will meet many new friends.